Chillona Chingona

poetry by a badass crybaby

Ely Lupe

DAXSON PUBLISHING

Chillona Chingona
© 2025 Liz Lozada
ISBN: 978-1-966337-05-8
Library of Congress control number: 2025907567

First Edition, 2025

Printed in the United States of America

Edited by Caroline Depalma
Cover Design by Sarah Crawford
Layout Design by Erica Castro

*Para las más chingonas, my (first-born)
first-generation ladies.*

You're more than enough, mija.

Author's note

Please be advised this book contains mentions of suicide, suicidal ideation, abuse, and rape. Individual poems do not have trigger warnings. Take care of yourselves, please.

As you will read, living this life has been nearly unbearable for me, which sounds dramatic as a mostly healthy person living in a first world country, but sorry, not sorry, it's my truth and it's really how I feel. I am more sensitive than the average person, so getting through each day can sometimes feel like a battle, and already having been through a lot in my nearly 30 years of life, I do feel strong and badass that I keep going.

I wrote these poems fully aware that many in today's society may feel some of the same things I do, so I truly hope with all of my heart that they help people feel less alone and maybe even provide some solace and hope.

One more thing. Publishing this book is a little bit like our little secret. Shhhh. I'm not telling everyone about it and I'm using a pen name not because I'm ashamed of it, but because there are intimate details in here that would scandalize my deeply Catholic and antiquated family.

However, I am happy to share them with you, stranger, just don't judge me, pls & ty.

Con Mucho Love,
Ely Lupe

P.S. I mention "God" sometimes in this book, and I would like to make it clear that I am not referring to the old man in the sky that religion teaches us to fear. I am referring to the force that created everything, ties it all together, and lives within us all.

P.S.S. All bilingual poems have translations because I wanted this book to be accessible to ALL first-generation women. The only one that is purposefully not translated is ESL4L, in order to convey the frustration I would feel as an English Language Learner.

Contents

---

1 Clean your room

---

2 Dual-income, no kids

Chillona Chingona

poetry by a badass crybaby

Part 1: Chillona

Chillona~Crybaby

I shouldn't be here.

My mom didn't want to have kids. She didn't even want to get married. (She wanted to be a nun. There's an alternate universe where that is true.) But in Mexican culture, kids don't typically leave the family until they're married, so she married my dad not even two years into knowing him, and less than a year into their marriage, I was born.

My due date was my mom's birthday, but the date passed and then, more days passed and I still wasn't ready to be born. Eight days later, doctors broke my mom's water and got me out via C-section. When I tell this story, I like to point out how they literally had to pull me out of my mom, against my will. Even as a fetus, I already knew that I didn't want to be on earth. I already knew that this world sucked, and I wanted no part of it.

Yet here I am despite that and despite my mom not wanting kids.

A true scam. Long story short, my childhood was ok, my parents worked hard to keep me alive (as they should), and I never needed anything, Gracias a Dios[1]. Food, shelter, clothes, shoes, school items, etc, were always taken care of, and for that, I am obviously eternally grateful. However, my parents failed to break the cycle of abuse, childhood trauma, and unreasonable, harmful expectations for their children. One of them was crying. I took pride in sucking things up and not crying every time I wanted to. But it got to the point where my body said that's enough, and I embraced my crybaby persona. Somebody once told me when we cry, we are also crying for all of our ancestors who held in their tears. That makes sense to me.

Anyway, needless to say, these type of expectations deeply fucked me up, but my parents are not entirely to blame; also, they made me the person I am, yada yada. I have been to therapy and I am working on fully forgiving them and myself but I am now stuck between the person I was raised to be and the person I am still figuring out. And my mental illnesses don't make it much easier to figure out, but I'm crying and trying, nearly dying in the process.

---

1 Thanks to God.

(Re)Birth

You already knew, didn't you?
Refused to face the deja vu.
This life really wasn't brand new.
Who the fuck would want a re-do?

They tore you out of your mother's womb,
born wanting to be in a tomb.
You didn't even care to bloom;
cursed to consume and live in gloom.

Working hard distracts like a drug.
I just want to give you a hug.
Get you out of that hole you dug.
I know you want to pull the plug—

better than living in a trance.
You really never stood a chance,
all you wanted to do was dance.
Same sad soul, different circumstance.

My mom says

Mija
Mi amor.
Limpia tu chiquero!
Eres un pingo!
Burro!
Te calmas o te calmo!
Tonta!
Mensa!
Melolenga!
Sope!
Pen-
Siguele!
Andele!
Ya ves?
La regaste.
Para que se te quite!
Échale ganas!
Ponte las pilas!

My mom says (English)

My daughter,
My love.
Clean your chicken coop!
You are a menace!
Donkey!
Calm yourself or I will make you calm!
Dummy!
Dummy!
Ditzy!
Dummy!
Mor-[1]
Keep going! (sarcastically)
Come along! (alternatively: you see what happens?)
You see?
You messed up.
So that you learn! (direct translation:"so that it [bad behavior] will be removed from you")
Try hard!
Put your batteries in!

---

1 Pendeja is a curse word and my mom rarely cursed so she would rarely say the whole word.

Who raised you?

So often—
too often—
in my adult life,
I ask myself that question.

Or better yet:
Why are you like this?
What made you this way?
I think of my upbringing…

afraid of any misstep,
learning to swallow my words,
carefully judge my thoughts,
forcing a filter in my brain.

Tienes que pensar antes de hablar.[1]

Persistently aware of my surroundings,
trying to remember to
occasionally come back to earth
from the space mission I was on,
because what if,

I'm in the way or
take up too much space, or
there's someone who needs help, or
I've been silent too long, and
I'm coming off as stuck up?

Tienes que poner más atención.[2]

And my manners!
Ya saludaste?[3]
I literally just got here.
Ya te despediste?[4]
I was about to.
And now it's awkward.

Ps and Qs? A given.
Se amable, se platicadora.[5]
Respect my elders? Duh.

---

1 You have to think before you speak
2 You have to pay more attention.
3 Did you greet everyone already?
4 Did you say bye to everyone already?
5 Be pleasant, be a conversationalist.

No seas maleducada. [6]

Growing up thinking
the worst someone could think of me
is that my parents
failed to "educate" me.

But people are out there making their caregivers look bad—
no— terrible.
Makes me sad.

I'm not saying I'm a perfect human,
I still fuck up a lot.
Pero some of you?
Se pasan![7]

And I have to stop my judgmental mind
my mom unknowingly expertly molded.

Maybe their caregivers did try, but they were ignored.
Maybe they didn't have anyone to raise them.
Maybe the person who raised them was just
doing what was done to them,
a cycle of people who were never proper-
ly taught how to be decent humans.

And so, we have a world filled
with people who are ill,
some who kill,
or have ill will,
and let it spill,
or take pills for the thrill
and/or to force themselves to chill,
and then have to acquire the will and skill
to finish raising themselves and hopefully be fulfilled.

---

6 Don't be ill-mannered.
7 You go overboard.

Limpia tu cuarto[1]

Just think about it.
How easy it can all be
for you and me,
if you were just disciplined.

Do you think I like looking like this?
An entire unholy mess.
But you couldn't care less
living in this abyss.

Ok you're right.
I know it's hard for you.
I know you'd rather it be clean in here, too.
But can you just try?

Like what if,
you just did a little, every day.
At least get the clothes out of the way.
You could do it in a jiff.

It would improve your quality of life
waste less time looking for things,
more time for you on the weekends,
overall, less strife.

---

1 Clean your room

Comer Comida de la Casa

"I didn't ask to be born Mexican,
I was just blessed."

As a child,
I would take a bite of my mom's
savory food, a perfect mix of spices,
textures, flavors, and love,
and send a thank you note to God:

"God, thank you that I was born Mexican.
Thank you that I get to experience this food on a daily basis.
Thank you that I have a mom whose love language is feeding people."
And then I would feast.

"I love coming to your house
because your mom is an amazing cook,
whenever I go to Melissa's house, she asks,
'Do you want a sandwich?'"

is a core memory for me.
Up until that point, I had not realized
how fortunate my sister and I were,
that not all kids had a mom
who labored
(and still labors)
every single weekday to
ensure that we had a tasty warm meal
to put into our bellies
no matter how taxing it was
(and still is)
for her.

"My sister and I are out of the house,
you know you don't have to cook for my dad
every day?"

"Yo no cocino para tu papá,
a mi también me gusta comer
comida de la casa." [1]

---

1 I don't cook for your dad, I also like having delicious home cooked meals.

Daddy Issues

Tu nunca supiste lo que es el amor. Y pues, ¿cómo te lo puedo exigir?[1]

The role of a father is vastly underestimated.
Similar to how most people
don't realize the monumental task
of being a parent.

They bring beautiful bright babies
to this world with their
emotionally immature asses
just to traumatize the hell out of innocent kids.

And then there's the patriarchy,
that never stops perpetuating
pain to everyone involved.
Yes, including men.

Y no soy malagradecida pero[2]

all you worried about was being that macho provider
making sure my mom had the
money to make a delicious home cooked Mexican meal
e v e r y d a y (except weekends) (which is still a lot).

(I wonder if you knew how incredible of a cook my mom was
before you married her. But, she grew up in rural Mexico, so you had to
have assumed with how our culture primes little girls to be "suitable" for
marriage. & I'm sure she told you she had been cooking since she was 8
years old, skipped the play kitchen and dolls for the real thing)

Anyway,

you made sure we never knew the feeling of a hungry belly,
even if our meal was maruchan and quesadillas.[3]
You made sure we had clothes and blankets and a roof over our head
so that we didn't know the feeling of being cold
with nothing to do to solve it.

But I rarely felt the warmth of my father's embrace.
Or affection or recognition
or advice or empathy
or emotional support.
<u>Just coldness an</u>d abuse.

1 You never knew what love was, so, how can I expect it from you?
2 And I'm not ungrateful but
3 cup of noodles and quesadillas

A ghost of a father figure.
A nutrient deficient meal.
A drained out pool.
A silent movie.

Even now, the idea of hugging you is weird and awkward.
Like hugging a cactus.
I stopped saying I love you
when I realized you wouldn't say it back.

And growing up, I tried to ignore
how it was fucking me up,
chipping away at my soul,
but I noticed it in little ways,
like how most of my close friends were boys.
It wasn't internalized misogyny; (maybe a little)
it was mostly me trying to find emotional connection in a male
presence.

(to this day I say a cis het man and a woman can 100% be just friends
because I have several high quality platonic relationships with men)

And let's not even get into
how I noticed it in college
(but I'm sure you can imagine).
Or how I'm bisexual but will most likely end up with a man.

But despite all the pain
and all the repercussions
of not feeling my father's love,
I can't harbor resentment.

Because how can I ask for love
and support
and empathy
from someone who
only
received abuse?

¿Por qué ?

¿Por qué me controlas?
¿Que no confías en mí?

¿Por qué me pegas?
¿Que no eres el adulto en la situación?

¿Por qué me gritas?
¿Que no puedes hablarme con paciencia y amor?

¿Por qué no me celebras?
¿Que no estoy aprendiendo como humano todos los días?

Si sé las respuestas de estas preguntas.
Todo lo que necesite, tu también lo necesitaste.
Y nadie te lo dio.
La toxicidad es lo único que sabes.

Piensas que me estas protegiendo,
que estas haciendo lo mejor por mi,
pero lo mejor sería que
comunicaras con el amor de Dios
del que tanto hablas.

Why?

Why do you control me?
Don't you trust me?

Why do you hit me?
Aren't you the adult here?

Why do you yell at me?
Can't you speak to me with patience and love?

Why don't you celebrate me?
Aren't I learning as a human being every day?

I do know the answer to these questions.
Everything I needed, you also needed
and no one gave it to you.
Toxicity is all you know.

You think you're protecting me,
that you're doing the best for me,
but the best would actually be
if you communicated with God's love,
that you talk about so much.

Wishing

I wish I wrote about more nice topics
the things I love and how I frolic

I wish all my poems were full of bliss
happy memories, like my first kiss

I wish my words only contained pure glee
but there is much more inside of me

I wish the world didn't make my blood boil
but humanity makes me recoil

I wish I didn't have dark thoughts in mind
writing about it helps me unwind

I wish that I had no need to heal
but sorry, baby, that's just not real

my head is my permanent home

it is the one that I've most known
it is the best one that I've grown
it is the only one I own
it is the only one not shown

but my head has a scary zone
at times it's hard to be alone,
inside, my home turns upside down
inside, I slowly sink and drown

sometimes I turn to stone
my life, I wanna postpone
I find it hard to hide the frown
I forget my head has a crown

it is the same one where I have flown
where I travel to worlds unknown
where I am able to disown
the one that can't be overthrown

In Space

My mom always called me
distraida,[1]
~Melolenga~
she still does,
because it's true.

I've always had a tendency
to escape into my own world
and leave this one for moments at a time,
and I still do,
like on this day.

I was 5.
We were at Disneyland.
I stopped to stare at the parade.
They didn't notice.
They kept walking.
I didn't notice.
I kept staring.
And thinking.
My mind getting
further and further away
from the present.
A spaceship leaving the atmosphere.

Time passed. I began to return.

My parents were nowhere to be seen.
My spaceship crashed and burned.
I ran around in a circle, looking for them.
I asked an adult if she had seen anyone with a
ponytail like mine.

A stupid question, yes.
But I was 5.
I was trying.
I stayed with the adult
until my dad and I locked eyes from a distance.

I ran to him as fast as I could.

I will never forget
my mom and dad say
that it was the worst moment

---

1 distracted

in their lives.
I was always made to feel bad about this moment,
as though I caused it
due to my spacey nature,
the exemplifying anecdote of who I was.

However, I recently realized
I did not become lost,
I was actually left.
Not my fault, but theirs.

Astrology Makes Sense

In a vast ocean
with turbulent, murky waters
live a crab
and a fish.

I, the crab,
have a shell
to retreat into
to protect me

and so
I learned to
dis-
associate

crawling into my mind
where I was safe
from the pollution
around me,

distracting myself
with my thoughts.

She, the fish,
with
no shell,
no choice,

had to withstand
the toxicity,
absorbing it
as it was the oxygen

she breathed
exhaling tears.

I came out when
it was safe again
or I was pulled out
against my will

back to reality

my sister next to me
coping
my parents still exuding
negative energy,

continuing to
soil our home
with their trash,
forcing us

to swim away
from the poison,
far enough to
one day

experience
clean, peaceful
waters, untainted
by their waste.

ESL4L

The old white Storytelling professor singled me out in class,
smugly declaring: *I can tell English was not your first language,
right? What was your first language?*

Spanish.

Yes, she nodded with satisfaction, *your accent has almost gone away, but I can
still hear it.* I sat there, dumbfounded that this professor thought it was a
good idea to say that to one of her students, in front of the rest of class.
What was I supposed to do? Congratulate her hearing at her age?

Pride won out all of the other emotions that day, in my mind at least.
I wished everyone I came across could hear my struggle to standardize
my Inglés in every syllable I spoke. My innate refusal to wash away mi
identidad. I also wished I had the language and courage to tell the old lady
off. I would have told her:

Soy Mexicana y American
with an emphasis on the Mexican.
Damn right the colonizer's tongue
did not conquer my mouth or mi alma.

My mother tongue
has allowed it to
vivir en paz, but only
porque nos beneficia.

Hable exclusivamente Español,
for five years before a single word of
English was forced into my mouth in Kindergarten,

         lloraba y lloraba
porque no entendia.
       it would frustrate me, frighten me
to not be amongst the soft, round, emotive sounds
that belonged to my family. I didn't want to, but I knew I had to
        assimilate.
A necessity, because my parents didn't risk their lives coming here for
nothing. Mi papá, a proud citizen of the US, siente gratitud y lealtad to a
country que nos quiere sacar. I can't tell him anything about the
country that gave him su negocio. After breaking his back his entire life,
he deserves so much more, yo pienso. Él y mi mamá lo dieron todo por
nosotros, y yo también lo doy por que se sientan orgullosos.

No one works harder than the children of immigrants.

Before I knew it, I was fluent, and with a lot of work from my 3rd grade teacher who wanted to rid me of the stigmatizing ESL label, I was "reclassified" to EO, to my mom's delight. Tragic

how replacing the "Second Language" next to English with "Only"
is a cause for celebration.

The English Proficiency Exam is racist, I tell my ESL students. They look around, and I watch it sink in. When they repeat it to other students and teachers, I feel like I'm planting seeds for the revolution. I make sure they are proud of their ability to speak two languages fluently. *You know they pay you extra for being bilingual and helping with translations?* I hope they do a better job keeping their Spanish than I have.

I know I should be thankful for being an "anchor baby," but I can't help but think about all that was taken from me by living in duality.
I am still proudly ESL, proclaiming it to anyone who dares make fun at how I pronounce unknown words phonetically.
Spanish sounds don't betray me the way English ones do, the way I betrayed my mother tongue.

While Spanish words still manage to flow out of me pretty seamlessly, there is an undeniable struggle that my parents and family lovingly make fun of me for. I make up words a lot.

I would have told that professor all of that, and finished with,
I wear the remnants of being ESL like a prize I labored to win and am still laboring to keep. I hope the glue that keeps those parts of mi lenguaje stuck to my English never wears out. They may have reclassified me to English Only, but yes, bitch, English was my Second Language.
I'm re-reclassifying myself.

perfect mexican daughter

an obsession
with perfection
a label,
placed & worn

"un angel"

a way
to survive
a cry
for attention

a little
affirmation
a lot
of pressure

please

a consistent
attempt
a decent
interpretation

an unattainable
goal
a ridiculous
assumption

a set up
for failure

didn't
ask for it
can't
get rid of it

never satisfy
never satisfied
excessive
apologies

Oldest Daughter:

Mija, you are stronger than steel.
I deeply admire you.
I hope one day you heal
from all you were put through.

All of the transgressions.
All of the times you put your needs last.
All of the high expectations.
All of the ways you grew up fast,

being the guinea pig
y el buen ejemplo[1]
dreaming big
paving the road

for others to know exito.[2]
Helping them find their way
because you know what it's like to go alone,
and don't want others to be led astray.

Thank you for planting seeds
while you were stressing,
so others would succeed
from you sharing your blessings.

All while carrying the heavy weight of being the oldest
with grace, asserting independence.
A tenacious, ambitious, perfectionist
never wanting to be a burden.

So remember to keep yourself at the top of your priorities!
Don't neglect your own needs
trying to people please.
Set and maintain your boundaries.

Asking for help and allowing others to care for you is good for the soul.
Don't burn yourself out.
Relinquish some control.
You are forever that bitch, without a doubt.

---

1 and the good example
2 success

A Wildflower

I was a good little seed.
There were no weeds.
They made sure of it,
had to save my spirit.

Fed me fertilizer, paired
with lots of care
so that I may bloom
despite the gloom.

They watered me,
Y crecí.[1]
I never felt old,
but ya estas grande[2], I was told,

when I was 10.
I didn't feel it back then.
I still don't feel it at 25 though.
Ya estoy grande, me digo.[3]

I just don't know what it means.
Should I eat more greens?
Will the world even be good
by the time I hit adulthood?

How will I grow?
How will I know?
Who will I be?
What will I see?

Will I survive?
Stay alive,
if I was planted
outside?

It's where I'd like to be, porfis.[4]

It's a lot of pressure
to fit into a pot
chosen for you.
The same soil kills a plant

---

1 And I grew
2 You're big now
3 I'm big now, I tell myself.
4 Please.

and what happens once you outgrow it?
I would rather be a wildflower.

Let my roots dig deep,
no longer someone's keep,
being me,
finally.

Never Enough

Unworthiness,
too many criteria.
I am inept.
Que soy muy seria.

My standards are high,
who put them there?
Did I?
Because they are
so much to bear.

I'm eternally in debt
trying to please
can't live without regret
I beg on my knees

for the voice in my head
la que anda atras de mi
que no me deja vivir
to pls leave me alone and
not fill me with dread.

You're so loud,
ya dejame en paz!
No me puedo oír
pero tu veras.

Un día
I will end my bluff,
no longer hand-cuffed
to those expectations
que ni fueron mías.

Que seas buena esposa
Que limpies la casa
Que sepas cocinar
"Ya te puedes casar"

Que vayas a misa
Que te planches la camisa
Que no tomes ni fumes
Que tengas hijes

No mas.
Quiero paz!

Unworthiness,
too many criteria.
I am inept.
They say I'm too serious.

My standards are high,
who put them there?
Did I?
Because they are
so much to bear.

I'm eternally in debt
trying to please
can't live without regret
I beg on my knees

for the voice in my head
the one that follows me
that doesn't let me live
to pls leave me alone and
not fill me with dread.

You're so loud,
just leave me alone!
I can't hear myself
but you will see.

One day
I will end my bluff,
no longer hand-cuffed
to those expectations
that weren't even mine.

Be a good wife
Clean the house
Know how to cook
"You can get married now"

Go to mass
Iron your shirt
Don't smoke or drink
Have kids

No more.
I want peace!

My thoughts, todos mios.
Unbothered,
Enough.

My thoughts, all my own.
Unbothered,
Enough.

Unknown

Era un angel
I am a stranger
Era un artista
I am barely a person

She was an angel
I am a stranger
She was an artist
I am barely a person

Le hecho ganas
She worked herself to pieces
Se quedó calladita y bonita
She kept it all in

She tried hard
She worked herself to pieces
She stayed quiet and pretty
She kept it all in

I fought not to tap out

I fought not to tap out

I'm not me
I'm not she
I don't even know
who she is

I'm not me
I'm not she
I don't even know
who she is

she got lost in
setting goals
reaching them
setting more

she got lost in
setting goals
reaching them
setting more

I don't know what I like
what makes me laugh
how to act in front of strangers
trying to please mi ma y mi pa
never learning how
to please myself

I don't know what I like
what makes me laugh
how to act in front of strangers
trying to please mi ma y mi pa
never learning how
to please myself

soy educada,
callada,
a veces creida.
Always anxious
I'll say the wrong thing.

I'm educated,
quiet,
sometimes I think I'm all that.
Always anxious
I'll say the wrong thing.

How do I act?
without thinking of
my reputation:
¿qué va a decir la gente?

How do I act?
without thinking of
my reputation:
what will people say?

She was a robot
but I'm not an actual person either
I killed her
now I'm a ghost

The robot malfunctioned,
so I killed it.
Now what remains?
A sad ghost of a broken robot soul.

Coming back to life,
figuring out the programming,
healing the soul.
Finding her, for the first time.

Where are you from?

Who me?
I'm from S-G.
That's South Gate,
not bad, not great.
Growing up, I couldn't really complain.
But I felt slain, let me explain.
All 'round me, in my community,
things weren't pretty, what a pity.

School to prison pipeline
taking away precious time.
Black & Brown kids
receiving harsh discipline,
but what can we do,
no one's listenin'.
Teen Pregnancy,
another travesty.

Lamentable
how it is so preventable.
Classes were 40 plus,
and most kids would just fuss and cuss.
Don't chu wanna marijuana?
To escape from all the trauma?
Go home crying to your mama
because of all the drama drama.

Acting, speech, and debate competitions
contributed additions to my afflictions.
South Gate was the underdog,
disadvantaged with the fog.
Inequitable school system &
institutionalized racism.
But wait Liz, back up a bit.
Back then, you didn't know about that shit.

That's right, but I had grit.
Other kids wanted to get lit.
Hey, not tryna shame 'em
because when they're 16, who could blame 'em?

It's all a lack of information,
oppression is rampant in this nation,
somewhat hidden;
intentionally written.

Now I wanna fight it
and right it but back then
when I was a teen,
I had a different dream.
And that was to expand my knowledge
by getting into a good college.

But since my parents had no money, my mami said,
Ely, honey,
I know exactly what you're feeling;
it seems like we're never winning.
But let me promise you one thing,
don't be discouraged by our lack of bling.
You just keep doing your best.
God and I will take care of the rest.

Fast forward a couple of years,
I cannot believe my ears!
Berkeley and USC
want to interview and meet me!
Both experiences were quite alike,
I felt right at home,
HaHa, psych!
No one looked like me or my mom,
being there felt quite wrong.
I looked around the reception room,
and then it hit me, boom.
The waiters were the people who
I related closest to.

From then on, I'll never forget,
my mission became the biggest one yet.
I would be the driving force,
I could be the best resource.
So that young kiddos like me
could feel that serendipity
fulfilling their life dreams.
So I'm thankful to SG
for everything that it gave me.

Where are you going?

My mind was aimlessly wandering
as it usually did in mass.
I looked outside at the sunny spring day,
which was easy to do, since this church had no walls,

the priest's monotone voice
at the very, very, back, like
the buzzing of a mosquito
bzzzzzzzzzzzzzzzzzz

the sudden long vibration against my thigh
took me out of my mind.

An email.

Discreetly,
I reached my hand
into my pocket and slowly took
my phone out.
My heart fell and ran as soon as I saw the subject:

Your NYU admissions decision

What?
Today is March 29th.
The decision wasn't supposed to be out until
April 1st.

I needed to open this, now.

I stepped out of the congregation
and the sun instantly enveloped me warmly.
I poked the screen to open the email that would decide my future,
skipped the first sentences with the pleasantries to:

"Congratulations! I could not be more excited to
welcome you to NYU."

Giddy with excitement,
I tweeted my acceptance, then
was immediately anxious
when I remembered what countless people had told me:

Even if you get into NYU, how will you pay for it?

My goal had always been a scholarship.
I knew I wouldn't be able to go to college without one.
With my heart still thumping in my entire body,
I checked my financial aid to find

over 47,000 in yearly aid.

Were they for real?
I immediately called to verify.
If you see it in your account, it's yours,
they said with the most annoyed tone.

Up until this point, I was sure I was going to USC.
Now I didn't know.
This was a dream program
in my dream school in my dream city.

I went back into mass,
now daydreaming about living in the city,
and debating my two options.
I had to tell my parents.
As soon as I told my dad,
he asked, te van a dar dinero? [1]
Mas de 47 mil al año, I replied. [2]
He raised his eyebrows

then gave me his blessing to do what I wished.
My mom, on the other hand, said:
Pero todavía vas a ir a USC,
verdad? [3]

The truth was,
I knew in my loud heart
I would regret
rejecting NYU's offer.

---

1 Are they going to give you money?
2 More than 47,000 a year
3 But you're still going to USC, right?

PWI[1]s

For as long as I can remember,
it was ingrained in me
to get some knowledge
and go to college.

As a first-generation Mexican-
American, I took the suggestion
as a requirement /only option/ surefire
way to success,

the avenue for acceptance
at their table.
My parents' perils
paying off.

Plus, I had the added perk
that I could liberate myself
from the prison my parents
put me in.

However, once I discovered
that tuition was more than
their combined annual gross income,
I knew I had to dedicate myself fully

to ensuring the burden wouldn't
fall on them.
And I worked incessantly
to achieve it, my freedom and

success pushing me forward.
This was it, right?
What everyone did?
What we were supposed to do?

Society did a great job
selling me a dream that only
half existed.
Imposter syndrome

yelled at me constantly,
when really,
I worked harder than a
majority of my classmates,

---

1 Predominantly White Institution

but still struggled to feel I had a seat
at an institution that was not made for me.
Was not made with me in mind.
Was not made to include me.

Felt the exclusion everywhere
from the classes, to the people,
to the professors, to the performances,
a constant reminder of

the many ways I was not a part of the dominant culture.

Sure, they could pretend to be progressive.
And they did.
But when it came down to it,
they weren't with the shit.

Refused to protect us,
refused to stand with us,
refused to change their ways,
refused to admit their wrongs.

And despite the fact
my degrees and the school
they're attached to have
and will continue to get me far,

I can't help but notice all
of the turmoil it took me to
get it. I can't help but wonder
why is this *our* goal?

Why do *we* force ourselves to
sit at a table that only uses *us*,
then ignores *us*,
and pretends it's always been with *us*?

We deserve *our* own tables.

II

We deserve them everywhere.
Because PWIs are everywhere.
Despite the definition only
including places of higher education,

most institutions in the United States
are predominantly white

and therefore it is difficult for us
to find truly safe spaces for us to grow in.

And because of the pervasiveness
of white supremacy
and the Western world,
it is not uncommon to find

them outside of the US,
their influences even reaching
parts of the non-western world,
despite POC being the global majority.

This is why we must build more
tables for ourselves in which
we are able to thrive and truly come alive,
where we can decolonize our minds.

My hope is that our tables will become
entire houses, cities, states, countries,
spreading seeds of freedom and liberty
ridding us of the status quo that has us in misery.

Astrology Makes Sense #2

I have a Capricorn stellium[1]
which means people often don't automatically see my soft Cancer center
and that's ok,
because those who have the interest to get to know me
will get to be enveloped by my deeply nurturing side.

I have a Capricorn stellium
which means I am hard working as fuck
and that's perfectly fine with me,
because I always have a fire under me
that keeps me going even in the most depressing of times.

I have a Capricorn stellium
which means I am simultaneously a perfectionist
and my own worst critic,
and that sucks,
because there is a voice
inside my head that won't leave me alone
about every little thing I do.

They say perfect is the enemy of good,
but I don't want to be good,
I want everything I do to be
e x t r a o r d i n a r y,
which causes me a lot of stress
but also success,
work ethic, diligence, practicality,
tenacity, and the need to plan,
so I can't be too mad,
but I'll always be on edge.

---

1 Stellium means you have three or more placements in a particular sign.

Anxiety

heart racing/ blood pumping/ hard
breathing/ mind going/ stomach churning/ slight shivering/ maybe
crying/ body betraying/ brain blanking/ brain buffering

sometimes for no reason

I don't want to speak/ I am paralyzed/ I watch my mind
meander/ I want to be alone/ not here/ not anywhere

i am sad. i do nothing

but stress

and then it starts all over again.

Depression

therapy sessions
isolation
distractions
emotions

dissociation

because it's sad to realize
what I see through my eyes—
the world cries and
a part of me dies inside

I'm tired of not feeling whole
the state of the world is taking its toll
and I'm losing control
I feel the darkness in my soul

in dismay
in disarray
all the signs my brain ain't ok
but I'm getting through day by day

takin' meds
playin' pretend
doin' what I can to mend
hopin' it'll end

Stuck in a Loop

Escaping reality to
a dark corner in my mind,
I'm losing myself in my sobs,
unable to stop the tears,

hoping to mitigate my misery
amidst the melting time
with an extended release,
then realizing

hours had gone by,
depression being
devoured by anxiety,
my fight or flight

feeling furious
with myself
for fumbling so
much time.

Self-loathing and panic
replace pity & pain,
my pending to-do list flashing
in my mind.

No, you have to stop having a breakdown, girl, you have so fucking much to do.

It reminds me why I
started crying in the first place:
I'm overwhelmed, exhausted,
and extremely depressed.

I start crying again.
I just want it all to stop.
But it doesn't. It can't. It won't.
I beg God to terminate my torture.

Pray that I don't wake up.
Choose sleep over the cycle.
But I do wake up.
& live it all over again.

Burnt Out

I burned my brain
I hate the rain
I worked too hard
I went too far

because I was discontent
and hell bent
on finding me
and being free

I was not prepared
I could not compare
I thought I didn't but
I was in it

A little lost soul
filling the massive hole
figuring out what fit
but I fell in a pit

of tireless working
studying dreading
worrying wallowing
crying wishing
it would all end

my brain told me
I'm done, sorry
I was not made for this
We were not made for this

Good luck
I would say you
can count on me
pero ya no.[1]

---

1 but not any more.

A Small Death

Existence:
eternal or not,
does it ever stop?
Sometimes,

I can't wait to get to that part.
You wanna go to heaven?
Of course! *But*
do you wanna die?

Kinda,
life's nice on occasion,
but mostly, it sux here,
doesn't it?

It's too much
and it turns my brain to mush
like I or we weren't designed
for this type of world.

Makes me wanna press pause on life.
Like, let me just log out real quick.
Turn it off, then turn it back on in a bit.
That's why I like sleep.

It's like micro dosing death.

A brief reprieve.
A release amidst the chaos.
A rest from the grind.
A respite from the world.

Until it happens for good,
and then who knows?

Hopefully permanent peace.
A prize at the end of the pain.
So heaven better exist.
If not, what's the point of this?

(S)easonal (A)ffective (D)isorder

I'm sad

sulky
apathetic
depressed

this
season
affects me in a
disorderly fashion

looks
so gray
and
dreary

it's
sinister
alarming
deadly

it
strengthens
augments
deepens melancholy

sun, save this sad soul
alleviate all this anguish already
drench this desperate damsel in distress

Poison

Cheers!
Sip, sip.
Chug! Chug! Chug!
Shots! Shots! Shots! Shots! Shots!

Unwind,
relax,
forget,
enjoy.

Let it lure you in,
alleviate you,
lighten the load,
facilitate the fun.

"Tequila runs in my blood"
I say as a joke
as I easily take back the shot
as seamlessly as drinking water

even though it's not funny
and actually true

because the predisposition
to this poison
permeates both
sides of my family

and I have seen it destroy lives,
cause trauma,
and nearly kill
my loved ones.

Treat the toxin with the thoughtfulness it deserves,
don't detrimentally use it to self-medicate in destructive doses.
It becomes a slippery slope from which
it's hard to recover. Trust me.

W(hole)

Fill me up.
Make me whole.
Be today's missing piece.
I need peace.

I want it bad.
I want it deep.
I want it all up inside.
I want to feel good.

Make me feel good.
Make me feel warm.
Make me feel wanted.
Make me feel alive.

I wish it would last forever.
Being present in bliss.
Needing nothing.
Feeling fulfilled.

Please

I live to please.
Your pleasure is my pleasure.
I am such a people pleaser,
I will suffer as long as you are pleased.

Allowing myself
to be coerced to do
things I don't want to do
just to please.

My heart strings tugged
hard enough
until they bend and break
to your liking.

Letting you invade me
after you say please repeatedly
even tho I responded no,
over and over.
Knowing you feel safe and happy
in here,
I put my feelings aside, again.

I don't look at you,
the man I love,
who says he loves me,
but can't control himself,
who would rather take the pleasure
instead of feeling it together.

I just lay there,
the piece of meat
you ravage,
waiting for the violation
to be over.

I want you to feel
an ounce of my pain
along with your pleasure.
You don't.
You exit, pleased.

Empty

I gave you all of me,
even when I didn't want to;
just to make you happy.
I did it solely out of love,

but it wasn't enough.
The loyalty, understanding,
unwavering support,
patience, abundant love for you,

the rent I paid for months
the groceries I paid for months,
I did it solely out of love.
No other motive, just pure love.

But it wasn't enough.
You said I was too different.
I was way too skinny,
I wasn't her.

And the betrayal hurt.
Especially from my first love.
I am so picky but
after almost 22 years,
although my brain said no,
my heart said why not make it work?

You were sweet and caring.
You showed me, with many actions,
that you loved me so much,
like planning the perfect b-day.
And making meals for me
when I was too busy or sleepy.

You were my biggest supporter
every single time I was stressed,
or thought I was being too much,
or didn't think I was enough.

'Til you came to the conclusion
that I wasn't enough for you,
and you stopped being that person.

Even though you knew you were the
only one I took home and had

the privilege of meeting my
fam and friends. Even though you knew,

not even a whole month later,
you cheated.

I would have married you,
I would have had your kids,
I would have been your ride or die,
you and me, til the very end.
I would have died for you,
given you all of me,
over and over and over again
'til there was nothing again and again.

That hurts more than the betrayal.

I lost who I thought was my part-
ner for life. My teammate.
The person who complemented
me.
I refuse to say other half
because that would imply
I'm not enough on my own but
I am.

Despite what you said and did, I
know I'm more than enough,
even after giving so much
of myself away to
you.

And that is what hurts most of all.

Knowing I gave myself to
someone who wasn't worth the pain.
Someone who took advantage of
me.
Someone who threw me to the side
when they found someone who they thought
was better than me, but I'm grateful.

I thank you because you taught me
my love is too precious,
and I shouldn't give it
to any asshole who treats me
decently.

I'm not sure if that type of love
should be given to anyone
except for myself, because
it's the type of love that left me
empty
with nothing to give, not even
to myself.

And now I'm afraid that someone
will take it for granted again.
I'm afraid someone won't find it
enough.
I'm afraid I will give too much
of myself, again, out of pure
true love.
So I'm careful.
Because I'm not ready to give
my love again. But one day, I
will be, and it will fill me up.

~

EPILOGUE

Karma
what goes around,
comes around,
good and bad,
She will make you happy and sad.
And it's only fair.

So I don't care.
I don't bother myself with feelings of anger.
I don't bother myself with plotting revenge
because you cheated on me in our bed.
I don't bother at all, and leave it to the universe.

That's what I told you
when you asked me if
I was going to call my best friend's dad
to come to the opposite coast and
kick your ass, like he promised he would
if you broke my heart, and you did.

And you didn't take that very well.
You probably would have taken it better
if I had said, yeah, he actually just bought his ticket.
But later, you told me how true it was.

That your karma was
desperately wanting me back,
and not being able to have me.

I could have destroyed your game console,
or ripped up your shirts
or chopped up your monthly metro card
or asked Juan to travel 3000 miles to fulfill his promise.

But something about
knowing the deep regret you feel
about losing the best thing that ever happened to you,
and regretting it longer than we were ever even together,
feels so much better than any of that ever could.
Thank you karma,
you are the baddest bitch.

Situationships

Commitment is scary.
Handing my helpless
healing heart
to someone else is…

yeah, no, I'd rather not.

I love me
a friends with benefits
and all of mine were A1.
(shout out to y'all)

Then it got old

& I upgraded to
~situationships~
because I'm
~traumatized~

& I needed to see if
whoever I was dating
was worth my time,
energy, and boundless love…
they were not.

& sometimes that realization
would hurt more
than expected,
& I think I know why:

in a relationship, you try it out, and it doesn't work,
so you break up.
In a situationship, all of that potential hangs over you,
like a ghost cloud, following you around, haunting you.

All the things we could have been,
if they had their shit together/ we were more
compatible/ it was a different time.
sigh
But I know sunny cloudless days lay ahead.

OK, I'll be vulnerable.

I hate to admit it
but
I want a life partner.

I'm tired of being
~miss independent~
I'm ready to
(occasionally and reasonably)
depend on someone.

I think I finally
understand the appeal—
why people seek
to make a deal
with someone else.

I don't care what anyone says,
life is hard
and it would be easier
with someone alongside me.

Someone to help with cooking,
cleaning, errands, my dog...
it sounds like I want a partner for convenience,
and I definitely do,
not gonna hide or deny that.

But I also think about how nice it
was to come home to somebody
and have somebody to sleep with
and just live life with,
ease my existential pain....

Ok. I think I'm done being vulnerable.

I'm Bisexual

As in,
I am attracted to genders unlike my own
AND my own gender.
So I crush on non-cis-men
ALL the time.

I dream of pulling them close
running my fingers over their curves,
kissing them, slowly, gently,
all over their soft bodies.

But it's kind of a secret.

My crushes have never
evolved past crushes
and so,
I have one foot outside

of the closet
because
some of my family
including mi mami

do not believe in the
human tendency
to have feelings for all genders
and we have enough we butt heads on.

So I am out
only in safe spaces,
but not being fully out
will always feel like

a betrayal to myself,
I've realized...

Chosen Family

Family is beyond blood,
not determined by DNA,
especially when that "family"
disagrees with the blueprint

beneath my skin

that I can't deny
that they won't accept
so then I don't come out
so that they can't reject

me.

While that's sad,
I am glad
I have those
who I chose

that love all of me
& give me the opportunity
to be free
in my identity.

That is my true family,
those are the real homies,
and we work towards achieving
liberation for every living being.

Consequences

It was necessary
for us to leave.
A reprieve for the soul
that cannot be still

in your presence.

It must be a different
type of melancholy
to live with the
consequences of your unholy actions

everyday,

as a parent
who couldn't get
their daughters to

stay.

Daughters who left
first chance
they could and
stayed

away.

Sure, we visit.
Partially out of love,
partially because
we feel we should.

Por obligación[1].

Trying our best
to not be triggered
by your toxic ways
and be ok.

---

1 Out of obligation.

Astrology Makes Sense #3

I thought I was in an 8 year rut.

Sick of struggling,
somehow surviving,
Tired of being tired-ing &
overanalyzing what was missing.

Was my mom right?

Did it have to do with leaving Catholicism?
Did I simply burn out?
Did it start with the birth control pills?
Did I deserve this somehow?

All of the above?

No. Turns out Pluto was in Capricorn
since 2008, which affects all Cardinal
placements, torturing us through transformation,
and I'm a Cancer sun, Capricorn rising.

Suddenly, it all made sense.
It wasn't 8 years, it was 15.
Starting from about the time
my grandpa died when I was 12,

through my pre-teen angst,
through my anxiety worsening
in high school and then in college,
through my many mental and
emotional breakdowns,

through my lowest point,
through my suicidal ideation,
through two Master's degrees,
through the start of my career.

I barely survived, but thank GOD
Pluto moved into Aquarius.
Fine, you're a planet!
Just leave me alone!!

You Deserve Better

If only
the world wasn't as awful as it is
If only
we didn't have to worry about food & shelter
If only
I didn't have to go to work every single day of my life
If only
climate change wasn't threatening our lives
If only
innocent people everywhere weren't being killed everywhere
If only
wars and prisons didn't exist

If only
I could recommend the human experience on earth
If only
I hadn't experienced suicidal ideation
If only
I knew the light would prevail over the darkness
If only
I could guarantee a positive experience on the earth

If only
I was mentally stable
If only
I knew I wouldn't put a lot of pressure on you
If only
I was sure you would never know trauma
If only
I didn't have a history of alcoholism and mental illness in my family
If only
I could raise you in a world deserving of you

My Inner Child

My little star, you're amazing.
Do you know I wish I could be just like you?
Life, love, and optimism for the future
can barely be contained in your small celestial body,

heart full of dreams
that you love to scheme,
brain full of thoughts
that would never stop,

with a soul so bright
and a sense of what's right,
seeking to share your light,
years ahead of your revolutions around the sun,

sharper than the cutco knives you sold to save up for college,
with the most enviable work ethic.
You never fell out of orbit.
You knew it was your way out.

Well, you did it, love.
All your hard work paid off,
You got to fly across the horizon,
and be free,

just like you had been
dreaming and scheming about
for years and years.
You fit the NYC atmosphere perfectly

with your ambition,
independence, and
insatiable curiosity.
I love that about you.

How tenacious you are.
How sure of yourself you are.
You know you are that bitch.
And yet—

you need others to tell it to you too.
You crave that love and attention from others,
but my sweet, beautiful, hard-working little girl,
move past this phase and
let your self-love be enough.

Love yourself with the confidence
that pissed so many people off.
You don't need anyone else to know,
YOU KNOW!

You know it in your heart, mind, body and soul,
all the power that you contain,
how mind-blowingly stellar you are.
So don't let them eclipse your light.

Dispose of the desire, the craving,
that became a need,
for them to recognize it too,
and tell yourself and believe it.

Stop seeking it.
Trust me, no matter what you do,
it will never be enough for them.
Accept it.

The star that you are is
SO MUCH BETTER than the space
dust they want you to be.
I know life feels lacking

without their approval but
fill that black hole with love for yourself.
We both know it exists in abundance.
Let that be enough

to keep you travelling forward.
You have already conquered many skies
and I know you have more to explore,
so go ahead and soar.

The whole universe is inside you,
waiting to explode.
Share your light with others,
before you implode.

Part 2: Chingona

Chingona~Badass

Blame my Leo moon, but I truly have so much self love, and I fully believe that despite being a sensitive "crybaby," I am, always have been, and always will be, a badass. Any (first-born) first-generation girl/woman can rest assured that she is.

One of the most badass things I did was move to New York City from Los Angeles at 18 years old with no family and no friends to greet me there. It was extremely difficult. After years of working my ass off, amidst working my ass off, I burnt out and my mental health plummeted. I began to cope in harmful, unhealthy ways and prayed for death frequently, every single day. I was a shell of a human being, wanting to disappear. But really, I wanted rest.

Eternal sounded appealing to me. The world wasn't worth living in and the life I was living wasn't worth living, despite going to a great university in the best city in the world and working on fulfilling my career as a teacher. But I was TIRED. My brain was DONE. It's a wild organ. It shouldn't want to kill you. Don't let anyone tell you mental illnesses are not real.

So, was I ever in danger of dying by suicide? Thankfully no, the thought of staying alive for my younger family members (shout out, Daisy!) was enough to keep me from doing it. Also, I was not inconsiderate enough to cause that logistical nightmare for my parents. After some excruciating years, therapy, medication, and transcranial magnetic stimulation, my mental health drastically improved.

I no longer want to die, yay! I came to terms with the fact that even though I didn't ask to be here and would rather have never arrived, I am here, in this agonizingly awful, sometimes breathtakingly beautiful place. God wants me here, despite me pleading for otherwise countless times. I might as well make the best of it. So here I am, trying to do that.

Since earth was turned into hell by colonizers, imperialists, racists, and capitalists, I feel I have the duty to try to alleviate the consistent damage being done, dream and enact better ways of loving and caring for one another, and live and love as joyously as possible, creating as much of a heaven for myself as I can.

Heaven exists in all living things and unites us all together. Experiencing that heaven, anywhere it is found, is truly magical. That heaven, which I saw and see in my life, is the reason I am still alive, and still a badass.

Omnipresent

The divine is everywhere.
But mainly,
the divine is love,
and is shown in the love
he/she/they/it
have for the world and
everything in it.

I know it can be hard to believe.
I don't think anyone hates the world more than me.
But if there's so much evil,
there has to be something to balance it out.
And I've seen that something
in a lot of places.

The divine is the sun and moon,
and stars and planets,
watching over us,
nourishing us,
ruling our lives.

The divine is the beach
the ocean
the mountains
the forests,
all the nature
we should seek to protect
and help flourish
just because its beauty exists
and sustains life.

The divine is in our friendships,
our relationships,
our loved ones.
Those with whom
we feel loved, cherished, and supported,
as we should be.

The divine is inside of all of us.
In that way, we are all connected.
All we have to do is listen to
the divine inside ourselves.
That voice. The intuition.

This is the God I have chosen to follow,
not the one I was taught to fear.

Not the one that punishes.
Not the one that condemns people for their identities.
Not the one that people use to exercise control over others.
Not the one that people use to hate others.
Not the one that people use to kill others.

But the one that gives us free will.
The one that loves and forgives us unconditionally.
The one that made us perfect.
The one that answers prayers.
The one that tells us to love each other.
The one that tells us to help each other.
The one that promises eternal life.
The one that lives inside all of us, and is rooting for all of us.

When we choose to ignore it is
when we may allow evil to leak
into the world.

God's Favorite

I have felt it was me
since I was a kid,
when I would send prayers to God
and they would be answered.

I would speak to God
and we would have conversations
and in the very rare occasion
when my prayers wouldn't be answered,

I understood.

A friend once told me,
"my grandma said
you can't pray for silly things like that"
after I told her I would pray on a discussion we had,
who knows about what. I was about 8.

I immediately knew she was wrong and I felt God tell me,
you can talk to me about anything.

And despite all of the trials I've been through,
and all of the prayers I sent asking to be relieved from living
that weren't answered,
I still feel like I'm God's favorite.

Because I am,
because we all are,
because we are all
a part of God's universe,
a part of God.
And so, we all matter a great deal.

If you want something, all you have to do is ask,
put in the energy, and God will come through,
as long as it's the best for you
and the universe.
If it's not,
I guarantee
something better
is coming for you,
because we are the favorites.

Thank You, Most High

Thank you, most high,
creator of our sky
and all that is,
for the gifts that nature brings.

Thank you for the crisp, clean, air,
the wind that goes through our hair,
providing us with the oxygen we need to breathe
and a much needed cool breeze.

Thank you for the abundance of water,
our lifeline, our purifier,
where we can also take a swim,
and explore within.

Thank you for the animals, trees, plants, and flowers,
that we can help grow and call ours,
and keep us alive,
as long as we also let them thrive.

You really said here,
it's yours, hold it dear;
it's all you'll ever need.
But some were blinded by greed

instead of the astonishing beauty,
choosing to treat it with cruelty,
so we shouldn't be surprised
to see the oceans rise.

But we still have time
to reverse the crimes
and live as one
before we are all done.

Prayers

If I ever need you, you're there.
You really care.

I've always felt it,
I still do.
I have no idea
what I'd do without you.

Especially when
I left the nest
and became a guest,
no longer in my home,
on a quest,

on my own,
you never left me.
I had a blanket to protect me
thanks to the all the prayers sent to me
by all the señoras[1] in my family.

What are prayers if not limitless positive energy?
A way to manifest what your soul needs.
How could I ever fall,
when with you, I have it all?

---

1 women

To New York

My favorite city in the world
that took in a young girl
who felt like she belonged in a place
consistently in a race.

Anything I want at my fingertips,
I'm able to free the nips,
there's always so much to do,
anywhere I go, I get a view.

I step foot in your grid and I lose lethargy.
We trade and transfer energy.
Brain whipping. Electrifying.
Life-giving.

And I love it.
Can barely live without it.
Depresses me that NYC
keeps going on without me, irrationally.

Makes me wonder
about the "jaded New Yorker."

How can anyone become numb
amidst the yums,
the rum-
bles everywhere?

Do you not care all that the city has to share?

The Greatest Country in the World

You could have it all/ a family/ a house/a good paying job/ a w/hole/
weekend all to yourself/ kinda
we call it the American Dream/ people come/ from all over the world
to experience it/ get their own/ nevermind/
how their countries became unstable in the
first place/ we were spreading/ democracy/ all

you have to do is give up your childhood in a school because
where else are your caregivers going to put you
while they work/ doesn't matter/ we're not teaching you
to think/ critically/
we're teaching you to comply/ obey/ be a cog

then/ either prove your worthiness/ exploit your trauma/ give up
even more of your youth/ in college/ be in debt the rest of your life/
go straight to being a part of the capitalist system/ no additional aca-
demic trauma required

and all throughout your life/ while you're working yourself/ to death/
you'll also be poisoning yourself with microplastics/forever chemicals/
processed foods/ fast food/ sugar/ it's in
EVERYTHING/ pesticides/ poison
in the air/ pollution from factories/oil refineries/car exhaust/ and

when you inevitably get sick/ we'll exploit/ your illnesses for money/
maybe you'll get a job with health insurance/ maybe not/ certainly
not our problem/ we'll probably deny your claim/ anyway
what matters is/ the pharmaceutical and healthcare
companies/ money/ not you/ getting better
we have the worst healthcare of all developed nations/ also

we know/ that you hear complaints from the poor/ marginalized/
but they really don't have much to complain about/ systemic
racism/ classism /aren't real/ their lives are not
harder/ more/ at risk/ just/ work hard/ you will be fine/

don't mind the cops being pardoned for killing innocent people
don't mind the fact those innocent people are disproportionately PoC
don't mind the mass incarceration
don't mind the fact those incarcerated are disproportionately PoC
don't mind the senseless/ deportations
don't mind the fact those being deported are disprortionately PoC
don't mind the injustices everywhere
don't mind the fact they disproportionately happen to PoC
they've always been there/ I mean what injustices/ what mass shootings
we can't solve/ because the NRA/ gives us money

you don't need/ bodily autonomy/safety/clean air/housing/free quality
education/ healthcare/better access/ better/ food/ food at all/no/
actually/ instead I think we need more tax cuts for the rich/ more
luxury high rises/ real estate/ super yachts/ private islands/ luxury cars
most of them/ don't pay taxes/ anyway/ do we
even need a middle class/a decent quality of life/ nah/ you just worry
about having lots of workers/ I mean babies/ yes/ I think the priority/
should be continuing/ to line
their pockets with more wealth/ than
they'll ever know what to do with/ weapons
for more war/ more oil/ more natural resources/ more wealth
to influence/ more elections/ laws that benefit them

who cares/ about the planet/ the increasing threat of climate change/ you
continue/ making us more wealth/ working
for way less than you deserve/ so those at the top get way more
than/ they deserve/ but it's not the rich's fault/ it's the migrants'
fault/blame them/ You just

continue/ being/ a productive member/ of society/ you're so lucky
you live/ in the Greatest Country in the World/ you're so free/ look
at all/ this choice/ Ooh/ Media/ Celebrity/ Culture/Wars/ Billionaires/
this could/ be you too/ just
keep working/ for your American Dream

Tiring

The tires go round,
I'm falling down.
They don't stop spinning
but I'm not winning.
Constant exhaustion,

I'll never be done.

And I'm so tired
I don't even dream.
And I am so tired
I really want to scream.
I feel like disenrolling.

But I keep rolling.

And it makes me wonder why
do I continue to try?
Exhausted means nothing left to give.
But we have to live.
What other choice we got?

Capitalism treats us like we're robots.

Impossible to reject.
Just tin objects.
No feelings, no soul,
soul-ly made to control.
'Til we have no use.

In a cycle of abuse.

Infinitely malleable.
Infinitely recyclable.
Infinitely drained of energy.
Infinitely in a state of lethargy.
Infinitely wanting rest.

Losing all interest.

We become a shell,
never feeling truly well,
just a long for the ride
because we're tied
to a system that does not serve us.

A system that is an incubus.

A system that benefits from exploitation
and indoctrination.
A system that drives the masses askew
for the benefit of a few.
And there's little we can do,

unless we form a coup.

Fight for the revolution.
Fuck the corporations.
Practice unification.
Achieve liberation.

Cycles

History tells us a lot.
For us marginalized, the lessons are depressing.
All that we've fought for the little we've got.
The ones in charge have made sure that we're always stressing.

We've seen it.
Upheld destruction.
They get you caught up in it.
Purposeful annihilation.

Their machine they built,
they're the real culprit.
But somehow we get the guilt?
Convenient, isn't it?

It's familiar maybe?
Perhaps we're lazy?
Cozy.
Life's rosy.

No.

It's not our fault
we're stuck in the same spot.
I refuse their default.
I hate the cycle. A lot.

A cycle caused by their racist policies,
inequitable education,
segregated cities,
and malevolent intentions.

The damage is vast
but we can learn from the past
make that shit last
& get rid of the caste!

But wait, I'm not done.
On top of that one
is the cycle of trauma,
ya know, the one we get from our mama,
that she got from her mama
and she got from her mama
and—
you get it.

Can't forget it.
It's imbedded,
living in our dna
waiting for the day
someone decides to breakaway.
Not repeat mistakes,
but alleviate the aches
that reverberate
through generations,
finally being the solution.

No longer ignore
the toxic sores.
Take on the chore
to try to restore,
and heal to our core.

If we don't, we risk falling into
a cycle of abuse,
accepting excuse after excuse,
finding it hard to break loose.

Accepting behaviors we're used to,
struggling to navigate conflict,
with little clue on how to
write a new, healthy script.

Breaking these cycles is necessary
for the recovery of humanity
as a whole community,
to give us an opportunity
for unity.

In SELA and All Over

When I was seven and my parents wanted to move
"to a better area," I cried and advocated
for a house with a for sale sign
across the street from my elementary school (sweet)
3 bedroom/ 2 and a half bath/ big kitchen/ pool/ Couldn't believe
my parents listened/ we laid roots
there/ can't imagine/ my life without/ being able to declare:

I was proudly born & raised in southeast LA/ in a hospital
in HP/ que ya no está ahí[1]/ Grew
up on the sparsely/ tree-lined streets of sunny/ South Gate/ Remained
loyal/ to the subpar schools/ and crappy education
while others lied/ to get into Warren and Downey.
Got conchas at La Favorita/ bolillos at Elizabeth's Bakery/ went
to el circo at Salt Lake Park/ shopped
en la Pacific/Tweedy/ Stonewood Mall/ visited
mi Nela in Maywood /Cudahy/then Bell/ Went through hell/ waiting
for food for an hour/ in the aromatic Maywood King Taco/ which
is the best one/ don't @ me/ best menu in the city.

Un burrito mojado/ salsa verde afuera/ salsa roja adentro/
un sope/ y una horchata grande/iykyk

Learned to swim and dance at South Gate Park/Ran
or walked around the perimeter in the dark/ a silent
celebration/ every time I saw one of the worn down
wooden mile posts/ Motivation emanating everywhere
because there were always so many people/ working
on their fitness there/ I never felt alone/ unsafe/ scared/ Threw
the swing over the rod
one time so my feet wouldn't hit the floor
while I swung/ so high
tried my best/ to not get shocked/ when I went down/ the slides.
Attempted tennis with my family/ my sister kept the rackets/ I never
got better/ sadly/ had so many dance performances/ my parents stopped
coming to see me/ for the longest time/ was completely unaware of the
golf course/ no one I knew/ cared/ it was there/ rejoiced
when the park finally got a renovation/ realized it
was because of gentrification.

Azalea was the epicenter/ Walmart was the omen.
Protests/ logical reasoning/ community complaints/ dissenters
traffic and environmental concerns/ failed to convince those in power /to
not build/ a large commercial center.

---

1 Huntington Park/ that is no longer there

What would happen/ to the small businesses?
The caucasity.

I left for college and laughed at the promotional video for SG/ where
it was transformed/ into a city/ I barely recognized/ pity
the message was clear: SELA was for sale/ My heart ached/ from 3,000
miles away/ knowing
the place I held dear was going
through a huge change/ wondering
about the damage they would pass off as progress/ thinking

the caucasity/ the influence of caucasity.

Thinking about how privileged I am to have a house I have called
home for over two decades/ people acquire/own
their little piece of LA/ and work hard/ to keep hold/ that I know,
only 2 units on the block have sold/ moved out/ each
time neighbors went to the open houses/ to see
how much/ they were worth now/ they'll let go/ the moment
it's lucrative/ convenient/ necessary
maybe. Even on our street/ the little pieces/ in twentyish years
have more than doubled (sweet).
My sister and I beg/ my parents not to sell/ so that we can keep
the home where we grew up/ not give it up
to the gentrifiers that already have taken so much/ of LA.
The real estate agents text me/ thinking
I'm my mom or dad/ asking
me to consider / selling
our home/ their chance at a come up/ a lawful crime.
My response is the same each time,
"So you can contribute to the gentrification of SG? No thank you."
No reply.

The caucasity.

Each time I came back for break/ more and more
had changed/ other LA cities noticing the same thing:
Improvements = displacements. I shouldn't have been
surprised/ considering
all the damage inside/ Echo
Park/ Lincoln Heights/ Highland Park/ Silver Lake...
I visit these places and I'm in shock/ at

the caucasity.

the amount of white people/ I see/ how
out of place they/ their shops/ look/ their ambivalence/ our pain/
for our cities/ fallen/ disconcerted/ about the future

of SELA/ anywhere/ they want to conquer/really.
The caucasity.

It enrages me/ the places Black and Brown people call home are being taken
over by people who do not care/ to keep
up the culture/ legacy that was lovingly cultivated
in the places/ they ravage/want
to strip/ away.

It enrages me even more/ this is not only happening in our barrios[2]
LA/ New York/ the Bay/ Chicago/ other
countless US cities,
but now in Latin America, also?

The caucasity.

It enrages me the most that destruction and displacement
is not enough/ they complain about
the places/ they are guests/ in
making salsas less spicy/ they can't tolerate
them/ outpricing locals and natives
out of their homes/neighborhoods/ trying
to gatekeep historic cities.

The caucasity.

These colonizers never fail/ to impress
me with their thoughtless/ selfish
conquests of places they had no hand in making/ condemn-
ing them/selves.

The caucasity.

---

2 neighborhoods

Betrayal

Proximity to whiteness has some of y'all in a chokehold/ because/
what's up with the self hate/ with wanting to look like the colonizer? do
you
not realize/ those fuckers/ raped and killed/ our ancestors/ violated
their bodies/ for us to look/ like what we look like now/ and

you want to look/ be /more like them/ you want to look/ down
on the people/ "con el nopal en la frente" [1]/because/ they
have less or no/colonizer blood/ you disgust me/ with your anti-Black-
ness/
your /anti-indigenous/ attitudes/ your siding/ with the oppressor/
your/ "mejorando la raza"[2]

you'll /never/ be white to them/ no matter how much you try to

erase our indigenous and Black/ roots and branches/ celebrate the colo-
nization/ that nearly eradicated our accomplished civilizations/ cling to a
made up identity/created to other us/then use it/
to other others

backstabbing/ our ancestors/ que con cuidado y amor [3]/took care/
of the earth y sus comunidades[4]/
came up with the foods/ we still cook
the music/ we still dance to
the traditions/ we still celebrate
the remedies /we still use/ para curarnos[5]
survived genocide/ for your malagradecido/a/e[6]/ ass
sin vergüenzas.[7]

---

1 direct translation: "with the cactus on their forehead" meaning they are evidently
Latine, whatever that means.
2 "improving the race" is a reference to encouraging Latine people procreate with people
with European features, not indigenous or African ones.
3 that with care and love
4 and their community
5 to heal ourselves
6 ungrateful
7 You have no shame.

In "School"

as a teacher I hear

I wanna go home
why am I here
will I ever need this in real life
most of these things won't truly help me

and all I can think about is how
they are right,
we are all basically wasting time and
it appears as though

no one thought about
how children actually learn
what would actually benefit a child
what is actually needed for a thriving world

no

all that matters is
caregivers being able to work
to be able to continue lining
the pockets of the rich

all that matters is
that kids are conditioned to
listen, obey, repeat
as we are meant to do in society

and they have to try and learn with

overfilled classrooms
unsafe campuses
burnt out teachers
tests upon tests
not enough nurses
not enough librarians
not enough social workers
not enough teachers
not enough community involvement
not enough resources
not enough care

but school police? sure

What about teaching them to think critically for themselves?
What about teaching them to advocate for themselves and others?
What about teaching them to be socially and emotionally intelligent?
What about teaching them, the entirety of who they are?

it is evident
public school was made
when child labor laws came into place—
if kids can't work

but their caregivers need to work
and eventually they will need to work...
it is currently the perfect place
to keep things exactly how they are

which is why the government wants to
get rid of the department of education
and critical race theory
and stop the (r)evolution of education

they are afraid of a truly educated population
who knows what they need and deserve;
having a (mostly) obedient workforce
benefits them and their rich buddies

so as a non-neutral educator,
it is my job to disrupt this system
as best as I can,
(until we build a new one)

by molding my students to be critical thinkers,
lifelong learners & advocates,
compassionate, self-aware human beings
that want to join me in making the world a better place

Doing Too Much

"Those who can't do,
teach" is a dumbass
saying because teachers
are consistently doing
and
have to know how to do
whatever the subject is
to be able to teach it.

And
on top of that,
plan lessons,
build relationships,
talk to caregivers,
attend meetings,
collaborate with colleagues,
be counselors,
motivators,
planners,
mediators.

And
on top of that,
keep track of
IEPs and 504s and ELLs,
make sure that we are
differentiating, accommodating,
modifying to reach all students.

And
on top of that,
do all of the things
necessary to keep us
alive and functioning.
so that we can continue doing.
All we do is do.

Vision, Dream, Philosophy

struggles, needs, set me free!
From South LA to Miami,
we all scream, no equity!

There's a lot wrong with society.
It's hard to not think it's up to me.
I feel a responsibility
to help out kids who grew up like me.

That's my vision, that's the dream,
that's what drives the philosophy:
the hope that our communities
will improve, socially, mentally, academically.

I will improve the situation
using culturally relevant education;
not to mention differentiation,
and lots of arts integration

to encourage student participation.
Students will do the facilitation,
analyze the information,
have important conversations.

They'll take charge of their mind's formation.
I don't want indoctrination.
But I do want to instill preparation
to be a part of this broken nation.

And what would that preparation be?
Critical thinking, boundless empathy,
finding our voice, cooperative collaboration,
and questioning the world's foundations.

Each one of my students will see
just how fun learning can be,
and that I care about their self-actualization,
I'll even provide the motivation.

And throughout it all, hopefully,
I will continue improving me.
I'll be forever improving education,
one day finally reaching liberation.

I wanna

I wanna be a creative.
Just create.
Help people
and help people with what I create.

I wanna be an artist.
Just make art.
Pieces that speak to people
and make people speak.

But I have to have a job
because I have to worry about
the roof over my head
and food on the table.

And it's hard when I come from work, tired
and I was already tired of living
and now I'm even more tired
because I got on my phone
and came across all the
terrible
shit going on in the world
and I can't believe I'm expected to work.

I wanna escape it all.
Wake up and not have to worry
about my 9 to 5.
Rely on the Earth, to sustain me.

I wanna go away,
live in the woods
or a secluded beach
somewhere,
just not here.

I wanna leave this country
that values productivity
beyond happiness and health
where we're clouded by the need to have the means to survive
and the pressure to be a part of the
downfall of late stage capitalism.

Mary Shelley wrote Frankenstein
when she was 19.
But what the fuck else was Mary going to do
in the 1800s?

I always feel bad
that at 28, I haven't accomplished
what she and others
did when they were younger than me.

Could I have written a novel/play/book in my teenage years
while I was in the
creativity-and-critical-thinking-killer-
babysitting-center they call school?
Maybe. I'll never know.

I remember being a kid
and thinking adults could just do
whatever they wanted
not realizing the (relative) freedom
I had as a child

then getting to be an adult
and realizing we have
the opposite of free will
the pure illusion of choice
a taste of freedom
amidst the forced labor.

I have succumb to capitalism
"yes and"ed a lifetime of work.
for a bit of "freedom" here and there when all

I wanna do is
create
make art
help people
vibe
eat
move with meaning
spend quality time
cultivate and contribute to a loving, sustaining, community.

Live in peace.

Vow

Doomsday/ a day set for doom/ a day
the world will go boom/ fire/ gone
like the planet Krypton.
Perhaps it's God coming down.
What if we all drown?

It's closer than we think.
The world is at its brink.
There's something about
how much some people crave clout,
how money is the honey,
and war is the lore.

Capitalism/ colonialism/ imperialism/ exploitation/ greed
are to blame. They pillage/ destroy/ the earth
is their favorite toy.

Will we win/ this game/ how
long will it last/ what is
in the forecast/ Honestly
probably war/ most won't endure.
This is what has won.
I fear/ we are done.

Can we overcome?
Is it/ the end/is it
too late?
Can we change
our fate? Who knows/ I'm stressing/ out.
What do we do now?

Let's say a vow.

Save ourselves
somehow.

An Ideal World

there are no borders
we treat each other and the environment with love and respect
we act with thoughtfulness & consideration
everyone has quality food, water, clothing, and shelter
no one worries about healthcare
community cares for one another
guns are non existent and unnecessary
people are rehabilitated, not imprisoned
mental health issues are treated with compassion
we allow others to live their lives as they wish
        (as long as they are not hurting anyone)
creativity is encouraged and thrives
"school" is conducive to learning beyond academics
rest is valued & honored

To Future Children

First of all,
I'm sorry
I or someone has forced you to be
in a place that does not deserve
you & me.

You see, the world we
are thrust into
has seen greed
overpower love.

The people that lead
were blinded by
money
and power,

intentionally
destroyed
mother earth,

and

despicably
exploited, tortured, and murdered
their own brothers and sisters

resulting in lots of
unnecessary suffering,
grief,
hate and violence.

So,

I'm going to cherish
all the ways in which
you are untainted,
a joyous unpolluted ocean,
sea levels rising
with love.

You can trust me
to be an aid through the
ongoing
increasing
natural disasters.

You can tell me anything.

I will put out the wildfire.
Save you from the hurricane.
Stop the landslide.
Be the water in the drought.

This love
and trust
will guide you
to becoming
a force.
One that outshines the darkness
and repairs the carnage.

This is my promise
and hope:
that if I choose to raise a baby human,
I do a damn good job.

I know I will not be perfect.
But I will hold myself accountable
and I hope you will help.
Because this
living
thing is tumultuous enough.

I would be devastated if I contributed to the
depletion of your resources
to survive.

Immortalized Martyrs
(Poem for Palestine in the Christmastime)

How are we humans not
comprehending the hypocrisy
around Christmas, celebrating
the birth of Jesus,
who was forced to be born outside
and whose parents were refugees?

How many Marys and Josephs are in
Palestine now, displaced
and trying to find shelter?
How many Jesuses are in
Palestine now, martyred?
How much unnecessary suffering
and death, to continue
to feed the greed of
the West's interests?

We can't even know for sure
since there is no limit to the evil.
Purposely starving the population,
bombing hospitals, homes, and journalists,
in an effort to erase their atrocities.
And so I am immortalizing their souls
in this poem.
All of the millions of people, throughout history,
who were killed and terrorized,
and those who continue resisting.
It is not much,
but we'll never forget.

The injustices committed against you
will not be wiped away from history.
While they're covering up
their crimes and
paying for more propaganda,
we'll keep fighting for you, Palestine.

Que viva Palestina y vivemos a ver una
Palestina libre![1]

---

1 Long live Palestine & may we live to see a Free Palestine!

Struggling yet Surviving

living with undiagnosed ADD among other mental illnesses is
like building with a busted screwdriver
cutting veggies with a dull butter knife
commuting around LA with a bike with flat tires
painting a mansion with a watercolor brush
and trying my very best with what I was given

does it get the job done? sure

signs of struggle but survive
make it work even thrive
barely notice the disadvantages but it's
agonizingly more arduous
exponentially more effort

taking tortuously more time

before I knew it, I was exhausted,
to the point I couldn't continue
with the increasingly broken and inappropriate tool I was given,
that was making it more and more burdensome

to complete the task and every other task

now that's not to say my tool is
entirely invaluable or irreparable
it has its use, and it is excellent
when performing properly
in its designated domain

so I had to ask for help to function in this world not made for my brain

treat it right
take therapy and medication
get enough sleep, food, rest, and exercise
use it the way it wants to be used, creatively and gently

and learn how to properly use the different yet divine brain I was given

Battling Darkness

We all are, at our core,
love and light. Nothing more.
But there is much hate and darkness
trying to dull our sharpness,
dim our shine,
and to our light resign.

As I became older and brighter,
not yet a fighter,
in an attempt to preserve my light,
I hid from darkness in my bright mind-

ing my thoughts and not
the murkiness and the rot
surrounding me, causing me
to want to flee.

I thought I was good just ignoring,
but I was subconsciously storing
it until it was pouring
out of me, following me around,
until I almost drowned

in the clouds and in my tears
wanting to disappear,
and give in,
let it win.

Paralyzed with fear
that death was near,
in disbelief my own mind
and soul were misaligned.

Do you know how scary it is,
when your brain
is constantly
working against you,
constantly
distracting you
and
constantly
trying to destroy you?

Distract or destroy,
those were the only two options

my brain would deploy.
I didn't realize though,
that by distracting myself,
I was also destroying myself.

Too scared to kill myself
but I was killing myself by
working my
body, mind, and spirit
to its limit
and not giving it
the love and light that they needed.

Not giving into complete darkness
was excruciating, every night.
I was comforted by the thought of
eternal peace and giving into the light.

I was truly at the brink,
no longer wanting to feel or think
or suffer, not seeing clearly
with so much darkness looming over me.

And so, having enough
of having it rough,
I illuminated my life
with therapy, and
listened to what I needed
to not only survive but thrive.

Everyday, I am so thankful
my world is, again,
mostly love and light,
and I have trained myself to not
distract from the dark,
but instead, make it into art.

Release

The emotions are rising.
The tears are on their way.
I know you feel like disguising
and pretend you are ok.

I know it's what you're used to,
to keep it bottled up inside.
But what good will that do?
It would be better if you just cried.

Accept the invitation.
Don't hold it in.
Give into the temptation.
Let the tears win!

I promise you'll feel better,
even though you'll also be wetter.

Maintain

I was handed a dry empty cup
that is not easy to fill or maintain
full/ to be honest/ finding the balance
between being charismatic and not saying too much

is a task I never cared for
accomplishing
but one that was consistently
pushed on me/ I would hear

"Calladita te ves más bonita"
pero tambien "Eres muy seria."[1]
Struggling to correctly acquire the liquid
society requires/ I learned

to not drain myself for others'
comfort/ it's exhausting being fake/ I'm awkward/
I hate small talk/ I would rather not
force myself to

speak/ if I'm not comfortable/
my brain is a desert
with no hope of rain/ but no one is harmed by
my silence/ choosing to remain sane/ however

if I am comfortable/ enough to share
my essence/ conversation will flow
out of me like the amazon river/ into
my cup, and yours
until our souls are full.

---

1 You look prettier when you're quiet but also you're too serious and quiet.

Present

"The present
is a gift,
that's why they call
it the present."

I never truly understood this phrase
 until I had anxiety and would essentially
force myself into the present using the
5,4,3,2,1 grounding exercise.

5 things you can see,
4 things you can touch,
3 things you can hear,
2 things you can smell,
1 thing you can touch.

Just being in the moment
is one of the
greatest favors
we can do for ourselves.

If it is an issue to figure out now,
then yes, be solutions oriented
in the moment,
and solve it now.

But if it is not,
let it go.
Gifting myself peace
instead of plaguing

myself with anxiety, anger,
and dread, focusing on the
moment, facing what is at hand,
being

p r e s e n t,

is the hardest and best life lesson
I am still mastering,
and a present I try to
give to others as well.

Take a Breath

Remind my body how it should work
when my heart races, my mind goes bezerk
my stomach does a flip and my heart sinks.
I have a feeling I have reached my brink.

What's happening is probably not that deep.
It's just, my mind likes to take scary leaps,
so I must remind myself to just breathe,
to calm what's happening underneath.

As a kid, I would replay in my head
what the Jonas Brothers said,
"Worlds are spinning round,
there's no sign of slowing down,

So won't you take a breath?"
trying to gather my strength.
Feeling my lungs expand,
reminding myself of all I can withstand,

because of the power I have within
that I unlock when I simply breath in,
and breathe out,
to get over the bad bout.

Transcend

There are secrets the universe holds,
intricacies that make up its mold,
waiting to be discovered,
asking to be uncovered.

My indigenous ancestors,
before most were sequestered,
learned and learned,
only for their secrets to be burned.

Thankfully, other secrets remain,
from which we have much to gain.

Amidst some of the worst professional years
of my life, I received a gift.
Transcendental meditation:
one of life's greatest creations.

A Sanskrit mantra is repeated
without being impeded
by other thoughts
but if they are brought,

"you innocently go back to your mantra"

I remember my instructor saying,
it feels a lot like praying.
You connect to yourself-
your highest self,
that self
that connects everyone
and is one.

Once you transcend,
you can feel yourself ascend.
Even mend.
I felt this was a godsend.

Which, technically (or mythologically) it is.

Sanskrit is thought to have been
spoken from Lord Brahma
to devas, to mystics,
deep in meditation.

Sanskrit, itself, means "perfect."
Its grammar is highly regulated.
Its words, expertly chosen
to match the vibration of the object.
Vibrations that have the ability to heal.
Afterall, isn't everything just the vibration of atoms?

Therefore, transcendental meditation,
in which a mantra is especially chosen for you
by an instructor after interviews and data gathering,
and you have an initiation ceremony,
and you sit for 20 minutes, twice a day,
and repeat this mantra over and over,
and achieve transcending from the business of your mind,
to pure consciousness,
feeling yourself vibrating to the original vibration,
becoming one with all that is,
is absolutely magical.

It lowers blood pressure and
risk of heart disease.
Improves sleep.
Manages pain and PTSD.
Increases creativity.
Decreases stress and anxiety.
Improves quality of life and brings peace.

I wish I did it more often,
because I do feel myself soften
when I am in regular practice.
But there's so much that distracts us.

Regardless, I am thankful for this gift,
and wish more people received it.

Medicate with Creation

Creating
is the antidote
for the sickness
I've acquired while
being alive.

A path
to reconcile
the duality
of living
in this magnificent
yet monstrous place.

A necessity
to make meaning
amidst the destruction.
An endeavor to rebuild.
My words/actions/
movements/dialogue/an
attempt to help
me and the world heal.

Instead of letting
the energy
out in a negative way,
I let the art take the pain
away/ in the midst of
depression/ nothing feels
better than a creativity session.

Tears falling down
my face/ anger slowly
being erased/ broken
parts of me coming back
together, happily.
The paper witnesses me releasing
my feelings and facilitates my healing.

Imagine
a world that was filled
with people who created
consistently/ let their soul speak
out loud/ shared
what it has to say
to the world.

Imagine
how much more
we would understand
one another.
Imagine
how much more
we would understand
ourselves.

Let's revive
ourselves through the life
we breathe into
our creations.

Purpose

Oh, what would I be without you?
(Nothing)
What would my life have been,
had we never crossed paths?
(a hole-y hot mess)

How privileged am I?
To be born with the gift/ craving/ need/ purpose
to share my heart and soul on stage?

How privileged am I?
To have been struck with
a somewhat exhausting portion of empathy/
the talent to emote it?

How privileged am I?
To have my path lit by my love for performing/ to know
my life's purpose at such a young age?

It was immediately fuck everything else/ this is/ what I want/ to do/
for the rest of my life.

Nothing compares to becoming intimate
with a piece of art/ sometimes
our own/ sometimes one that came from a kindred
spirit/ someone else who acted
on the impulse to share/ themselves
with the world.

Nothing compares to embodying a character/ becoming
someone else for a given period of time/ feeling
their experiences/ sharing
it so others experience it too, or not/
(there's a reason why role playing is widely used/ therapeutic
method/ a way some choose to spice up/ their sex/ lives.)

Nothing compares to collaborating with others/ on a shared vision/ mis-
sion to bring this piece of soul to life/ a process that creates/
families/ if nourished correctly/ a process
that can move me to tears/ with its beauty/ it(')s
synergistic/ essence/ harmonious

Nothing compares to beings on stage/ in conjunction/ with lights/
sound/ music/ objects from everyday life/ or made/ up/ set created with
a combination of nature and humanity's advancements/ everything con-

jured carefully, with consideration/ cooperation/ conversation/
creativity/ our souls working as one/ to give birth.
Sharing our creation live/ in real time/ to an audience hungry
for the culmination of the combination of all the minds/ souls/ moving
parts/ working/ together seamlessly/ Energy

flowing throughout the room, being transferred from performer
to spectator/ back and forth/ telepathically
until it's over/ the audience buzzing...
conversation and thoughts/ expanding
their expertise on existence.

It's a ritual we've always been drawn to/ hearing/ learning
from one another/ together/ on our own/ a way to unity.
It's a ritual I am proud of/ continuing/ passing on to students.
It's a ritual that will always live in my soul/ in every lifetime/
in every universe/ my first love.

Long Beach Beach

sea debris
carry me
floating free
happily

floating away
catching some rays
riding a wave
storms will be braved

what will remain?
what will be gained?
will the pain
be in vain?

what will I mean?
being weaned
being cleaned
no longer seen

Clear Sunny Skies

I'm a summer baby,
PROUDly born in the month of June.
My mom says I was born on a cloudless day.
My favorite.

I like staring
into the vast, infinite, blueness.
It makes me feel…
miniscule,

reinforces my existentialism,
and my belief we're not alone
in this universe so large…
nothing matters.

Only this present moment

when the sun can
liberally shine bright
on my skin with
nothing in its way.

I close my eyes and take it in,
the sun's energy enveloping me
and eradicating my issues,
like it did to the clouds.

All of a sudden
life has meaning again,
and I thank the Creator
for the moment.

I want to be that free,
bright, and uninterrupted.
I want to be that warm
and nourishing,

endlessly.

I love my friends

I love my friends.
I don't have a lot
but the ones I do have
have my whole heart.

I love my friends.
Not bound by blood,
or by the law,
but forever buds.

I love my friends.
Relationships may come and go,
but a quality friend
helps you grow.

I love my friends.
Carefully chosen,
our entire lives
lovingly interwoven.

I love my friends.
I got them,
they got me,
such gems.

MAYA

My why, my wild joy
You may not survive sans me
Sans you, I'm destroyed

4:20

This is a poem
about weed.
It's not like
I need

it('s)
just nice
I don't have to
think twice.

Just fill
my bowl, have a chill
little break
for goodness sake!

It is one of the greatest gifts
of the universe, that lifts
us to great high(ts)
and insights,

brings people together
no matter the weather
gets them sharing
and caring
and loving
and eating
and sleeping
and talking
and listening
and vibing
and hanging
and feeling

or not,
that's cool too.

I remember the first time I smoked weed. It was my first Halloween in NYC. I had one of the greatest nights. I was crossfaded.

I love being crossfaded,

but smoking cannabis is looked down upon in some of my circles, so I can't be crossfaded very often

which is probably a good thing.

I'm not the most functional person. I'm already cursed to living life a little lost. The highness elevates it. I only see clearer in some ways.

So you may ask, like my mom does, why make it worse?

But just like it enhances my spaciness, it enhances everything else, good or bad, obviously, so I must use it with caution. People can have their daily habits with cannabis. That's cool.

That life, sadly, no longer serves me well. But it's ok, I smoke socially and sometimes creatively.

Living the DINK[1] Life

For Gabe

I've never felt this way before,
you have weirdly changed my lore.
Never would I have thought that I would,
feel that I could,
maybe should,
dedicate my life
to be your stay at home wife.

Now, that is not happening.

But just having the feeling
of that kind of life being appealing
sends me reeling,
makes me feel like concealing
that my brain goes there
without a care.

And this is not
a cheap shot.
I'm not hating on those
who chose to do so.
In fact, I now understand
why someone might wanna
do that for their man.

See for me,
I wanna cater to your every need,
and I want it to be my creed.
I want my life to
(partially)
revolve around you,
and hey, not working
would be nice, too.

But there's too much I wanna do.
And I love our DINK life, boo.
And I must have my own money,
So I'll just fantasize about it, honey.

---

1 Dual-Income, No Kids

Sources of Strength

I am strong
on my own
but I am not
alone.

I never have to
rely on just me
and that makes
me so happy.

It gives me hope
fortifies my resilience
gives me endurance
to develop my brilliance.

Ever Evolving

how long will it be
how long will you be
healing from within
healing from the sins

it's been 10 Junes
since you
flew the coup
off to pursue

freedom
needed some
and to become
someone

who
I grew
anew
renewed
in lieu
of who
they subdued
and construed

incorrectly
I am not she
she was not free
she had to flee
did not forsee
how hard it would be
to truly be free

to find peace

in a place
in a race
in a chase
common place

to screw
those who
outgrew
the untrue
brew

that they feed
to mislead
make you need
feed greed
heed creeds
go "succeed"
just concede.

So
I know you
flew askew
lost site of the view

but now you need to
follow through,
continue to
pursue
the real you

and
go debut
who you grew
maybe a bit taboo
but nevertheless true-
ly you.

The Real Me

I'm baffled by people who
are able to be 100% themselves
100% of the time.
Because first of all,
I don't even know who I am.
I envy y'all.

And sometimes, it is simply not possible for me.
The real me never fucking wears a bra
and always fucking curses.
But can I do either at my job as a teacher? Naw.

I don't curse in front of my mom either,
por respeto, [1]
and she doesn't let me and my lil titties be great
but we do anyway.
Also, she doesn't know I'm not straight.

Because even though I'm bi,
I love dick too much and
I'll probably end up with a guy,
so why even invite that fight?

I can already hear her saying,
entonces nada más eres promiscua? [2]
Which, yes, the real me also is, but I reign her in.
Entonces déjame en paz, ma. [3]

And it's not just her.
I also worry about
being too me
with my colleagues,
being a role model
with my students and my family
and not being too
nihilistic and shady.

So I stay quiet a lot.

And I had come to terms
with this being my life
with being this different person
with my dog

1 Due to respect
2 So you're just promiscuous?
3 So, leave me alone, mom.

with my friends
with my family
with my students
with my students if admin is present
with my colleagues
and by myself
and I was ok with that...

but now
I'm publishing a book,
which terrifies me
because then aspects of the real me
that some people have never seen
will be seen for the first time
and they'll react as if I've committed a crime.
That "professional"
that teaches class
that girl that was raised Catholic
and read in mass
will be revealed to be...me.
Whoever that is.

Bi.
Radical.
Sexual.
Crass.
Shady.
Nihilistic.

But still!

Empathetic.
Caring.
Smart.
Strong.
Loving.
Optimistic.

In the end, still me.

Whoever that is.

Golden

Twenty-nine on the twenty-ninth;
I feel more than fine.
Child of the moon,
you'll be thirty soon.

Enjoying my twenties for one more year.
Years I cried tears struggling towards
and achieving the next goal, and the next goal
hoping it would be the one to make me feel whole.

I think I'm getting there,
I'm treating my body with more care,
keeping my mental illnesses in check,
no longer a hopeless wreck. Still kind of a mess,

but growth is not linear
and I no longer feel inferior.
I will take my wins, and I'm so excited
for this golden era of my life to begin.

Farewell

To my 20s

a decade I
started begrudgingly surviving, ended mostly thriving.
started so broke I could barely eat, ended living comfortably
started with my mental health hanging by a thread, ended regulated
started a lost soul in NYC, ended a soul in perpetual evolution in LBC
started w/ an underdeveloped pre-frontal cortex, ended with it developed
(solved a lot of problems)

To my 20s
the decade filled with
learning/questioning/growing/grinding/ healing/ loving/ creating/
moving
travelling/ discovering/ crying/ fighting/ struggling/ accomplishing/
(truly exhausting)

To my 20s
this decade was
hard as fuck
fun as fuck
eye-opening as fuck
heart-shattering as fuck
unlivable as fuck
incomparable as fuck
(I would never want to relive them, the fuck?)

To all my 20-somethings, the world is unfair,
please take care.
Take it from me, I barely made it out alive...
and can't wait to be in my thirties and thrive.

Chillona Chingona

Crecí tratando de no chillar
cuando sus ojos decían "deja de chingar,"
y reprimiendo chillidos
cuando aguantaba chingadazos.

De vez en cuando sí chillaba,
especialmente cuando me sentía bien chingada en la escuela,
como la vez que chillé porque no me chingué el examen
y siempre me los chingaba.

Siempre andaba en chinga
de un lado para otro, ocupada.
Mis papas me decian chiquilla callejera,
pero usualmente era para la escuela.

Me sentía muy chingona
en ese estilo de vida, trabajadora,
sin ser chillona
pero esa persona no era sana.

Casi llegué a matarme.
Tope con mi limite y me dije,
Chillare para sanarme,
ya no me chingare aguantándome.

En los últimos años he chillado un chingo
y chillo cuando quiero, por cualquier chingadera.
Todavía me chingo trabajando
pero ahora con más cuidado.

Me siento más chingona que nunca
por aceptarme como persona chillona,
sentirme fuerte en mi vulnerabilidad,
sobresalir en mis metas y seguir la lucha.

Chillaria y chingaria mucho menos
si el mundo no estuviera tan chingado,
pero por eso sigo chillando hasta sentir calma
y chingando con toda mi alma

para no decirles a todos que...

Badass Crybaby

I grew up trying not to cry
when your eyes said "stop bitching"
and holding back cries
as I withstood hitting.

Every now and then I would cry,
especially when I felt fucked in school
like the time I cried because I didn't ace the exam
and I always aced them.

I was always in a hurry
from one place to another, busy.
My parents called me street girl
but it was mostly for school.

I felt super badass
living this kind of life, hardworking,
without being a crybaby
but that person wasn't healthy.

I almost killed myself.
I hit my limit and I told myself
I will cry to heal,
I will no longer fuck myself over holding it in.

In recent years, I have cried a shit ton
and I cry whenever I want, for any little thing.
I still fuck myself over working,
but now with more care.

I feel more badass than ever
now that I have accepted my crybaby persona,
found strength in my vulnerability,
surpass my goals, and keep fighting.

I would cry and bitch a lot less
if the world wasn't as fucked as it is
but that's why I'll keep crying until I feel calm,
and fucking with my whole soul,

so I won't tell everyone to...

Acknowledgments

Thank you to the higher power that exists everywhere and made everything including me (sigh) and guides me through life.
Thank you to my loved ones that remind me this higher power exists.

> Gabe, for consistently making my life easier & infinitely more enjoyable. I love the life we live.
> Daisy, for being my reason to stay alive. You make me so proud.
> Oriana, for being the literal reason I am alive. I would not have survived NYU or NYC without you.
> Andres, for being a supportive, loving friend through all my phases since '06.
> Lulu, for surviving my childhood with me and still being here.
> Francesca, for reading all of my things and going to Da Poetry Lounge with me so many times and being an amazing friend.
> Laura, for being my gemelita,[1] and such a safe, warm, fun space.
> Breial, for being an example of God's love. I wanna be like you when I grow up!
> Melvin, for being a great listener and for the memes and videos that still keep me afloat.
> Hector, for all the judgment-free advice since high school.
> Brittney, for dreaming and being an artist with me.
> Jocelyn, for all the encouragement and heartfelt conversations.
> Mi familia,[2] for all the love and support & being my village.
> My teachers who inspired me to be like them.
> (SE) LA[3] for raising me.
> New York for finishing the job.
> The CLI Long Beach Chapter for all our inspiring Saturday sessions, Tommy and Kimiko for their unwavering continuous guidance and suppport, and Grace for being a friend in poetry & life.
> My students, for making me love my job and being a future I can look forward to.
> Maya, for being the light of my life. I love you, honey buns.
> & a HUGE thank you to my publisher, Erica for helping me amplify my voice! Could not have done this without you.

Thank you to me! For keeping me alive even when shit got rough and getting through late stage capitalism one day at a time.
And thank you to you, who read this book! I hope with all my heart you enjoyed, laughed, and maybe even cried with me.

---

1 Twin
2 My family
3 Southeast Los Angeles

Author Bio

Ely Lupe is the first-born daughter of two Mexican immigrants. She was born and raised in Southeast LA, attended New York University, and acquired a Dual Master's degree in Educational Theatre and English Education. She has acted on stage, written, directed, and produced theater, and recently had a play put on at Frida Kahlo Theater's 10 Minute Play Festival. Her poem, *Long Beach Beach* was published in the anthology, *Long Beach Spits Fire.* She is currently living the dream, teaching theater to high school students. She aspires to one day do so outside of the traditional school system while continuing to create art for the page and the stage. You can follow her on instagram @elylupe_.

Publisher's Note

Daxson publishing was created to help marginalized artists publish their work, so the world can hear their voice. The vision for this publishing house is to help people get their work out there, and not have them struggle finding their way through the publishing process. Everyone's voice deserves to be heard, and we are here to help. If you are interested in submitting a manuscript, email daxsonpublishing@gmail.com. Support our cause! Buy our books at daxsonpublishing.com.

www.ingramcontent.com/pod-product-compliance
Lightning Source LLC
Chambersburg PA
CBHW031424120626
46545CB00006B/2260